The End of the American Revolutionary War

The Colonists Defeat the British at Yorktown

Allison Stark Draper

PowerKids Press ™

New York

For my father

Published in 2001 by The Rosen Publishing Group, Inc.
29 East 21st Street, New York, NY 10010

Copyright © 2001 by The Rosen Publishing Group, Inc.

First Edition

Book Design: Michael de Guzman

Photo Credits: pp. 5, 9, 15, 18, 21 © North Wind Pictures; p. 6 © Archivo Iconografico, S. A./CORBIS; p. 11 © Bettmann/CORBIS; p. 12 © CORBIS; p. 17 by Michael de Guzman.

Draper, Allison Stark.
    The battle of Yorktown / by Allison Stark Draper.— 1st ed.
       p. cm.— (Headlines from history)
    Includes index.
    Summary: Briefly surveys the Revolutionary War and describes the battle at Yorktown which forced the British to surrender and ended the war.
    ISBN 0-8239-5674-1 (alk. paper)
    1. Yorktown (Va.)—History—Siege, 1781—Juvenile literature. [1. Yorktown (Va.)—History—Siege, 1781. 2. United States—History—Revolution, 1775–1783—Campaigns.] I. Title.

E241.Y6 D73 2000   00-024771
973.3'37'09755423—dc21

Manufactured in the United States of America

CONTENTS

1	American Colonists Want Freedom From British Rule	4
2	France Helps American Colonists Fight British	6
3	British Beat Americans in Georgia and South Carolina	8
4	Americans Win Battle at King's Mountain	10
5	Americans Force British Army to Head North	12
6	French Navy Wins Battle Against British	14
7	Americans and French March on Yorktown	16
8	Americans Trap British at Yorktown	18
9	British Surrender to Americans	20
10	American Colonies Become States	22
	Glossary	23
	Index	24
	Web Sites	24

American Colonists Want Freedom From British Rule

In the 1600s, England founded 13 **colonies** in America. People from England moved to these colonies. The colonists lived in America, but they were still **subjects** of the English king. This meant they had to obey English laws and pay money to the English government.

Over the years, the colonists started to think of themselves as more American than English. They were tired of having to obey the English government. By the late 1700s, the Americans were ready to rule themselves.

The English did not want the colonists to be free. They

No one is sure whether the Americans or the British fired the first shot at the Battle of Lexington.

4

wanted to control the money and land in the colonies. King George III, the king of England at the time, sent British soldiers to control the Americans. The Americans did not give in. They fought for their freedom. In 1775, there were battles in the cities of Lexington and Concord, Massachusetts. These battles between the Americans and the British started the Revolutionary War.

5

France Helps American Colonists Fight British

The colonists needed soldiers and money to fight the Revolutionary War. They turned to France for help. France had lost the French and Indian War to England in 1763. The French thought of the English as enemies, but were afraid to help the

6

Americans. The French did not think the Americans had enough soldiers to beat the British.

On October 17, 1777, the Americans won a battle against the British at Saratoga, New York. This was an important battle because it proved to the French that the Americans could beat the British. The French sent soldiers and money to help the Americans. A French general named Lafayette won many battles for the Americans. He and General George Washington became close friends. Washington was in charge of the American army. Another Frenchman named General Rochambeau brought 6,000 French soldiers to America to help fight the British. An admiral in the French navy named de Grasse brought a **fleet** of French ships.

General Lafayette was a close friend of George Washington. When Lafayette had a son, he named him after Washington.

British Beat Americans in Georgia and South Carolina

General Charles Cornwallis was in charge of the British troops in the American South. In the fall of 1778, General Cornwallis took over the city of Savannah, Georgia. In May 1780, Cornwallis attacked Charleston, South Carolina. On May 12, 1780, the British forced the Americans to **surrender**.

General Cornwallis and his British soldiers marched north. The Americans wanted to stop Cornwallis before he reached North Carolina. In July 1780, American general Horatio Gates led 4,000 American soldiers in a battle against

8

Cornwallis's 2,300 British soldiers. The two armies fought at Camden, South Carolina, on August 16, 1780. The British beat the Americans again.

With General Cornwallis as their leader, the British troops won battles against the Americans in Georgia and South Carolina.

9

Americans Win Battle at King's Mountain

Losing battles to the British made the Americans fight even harder. American colonists in South Carolina attacked British **messengers** and storehouses.

Francis Marion was one of the leaders of the American troops in the South. Marion was called the "Swamp Fox" because he knew a lot about South Carolina's swampy forests. The British had trouble fighting against men like Marion in the **wilderness**.

The Americans beat the British at King's Mountain in the colony of South Carolina. This map shows the 13 colonies.

10

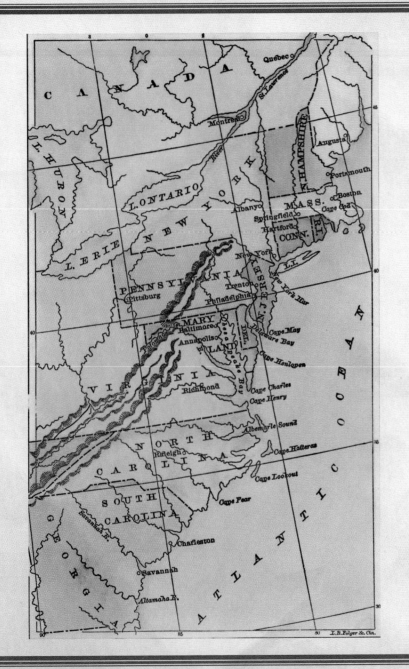

In 1780, a British major named Patrick Ferguson decided to attack the Americans in the southern wilderness. A group of American soldiers went to fight him. On October 7, 1780, they surprised Ferguson and his British soldiers at King's Mountain in South Carolina. They killed Ferguson and most of his men.

11

Americans Force British Army to Head North

In December 1780, American general Nathanael Greene became the leader of the American army in the South. Greene led many small attacks on the British. On January 17, 1781, an

12

American general named Daniel Morgan led an attack against the British at Cowpens, South Carolina. The Americans won the battle against British general Cornwallis and his soliders.

General Greene marched north ahead of Cornwallis. Greene had 4,500 men. Cornwallis had only 2,200. On March 15, 1781, the British arrived in North Carolina. The Americans attacked. Cornwallis lost 532 men. He decided to **retreat** to Yorktown, Virginia.

American general Daniel Morgan led a successful attack against the British in South Carolina. The battle took place on January 17, 1781.

French Navy Wins
Battle Against British

In the spring of 1781, American general George Washington was in New York. One of his **allies**, General Lafayette, was in Virginia. Lafayette told Washington that General Cornwallis was in Yorktown, Virginia. Washington decided to attack Cornwallis and his men in Yorktown. He had help from two other French allies. Admiral de Grasse sailed to Virginia with 29 French warships. General Rochambeau joined Washington with 6,500 soldiers.

On August 21, 1781, Washington and Rochambeau marched south with 7,000 men. On September 2, de Grasse

After the British fleet was damaged, the British retreated to New York.

sailed into Virginia's Chesapeake Bay. A British fleet came from New York on September 5. The French attacked the British. The French fleet damaged some British ships. The British retreated to New York. They knew they could not beat the French with so few ships left. The French now controlled Chesapeake Bay.

15

Americans and French March on Yorktown

In September of 1781, the American and French armies marched from Rhode Island to Yorktown, Virginia. The march to Virginia was almost 500 miles. The Americans knew that the British had a **fort** in Yorktown. American general Washington and French general Rochambeau planned a **siege** against the British. They dug deep **trenches**.

Inside the fort, British general Cornwallis was worried. He had about 7,500 men. Together, the Americans and French had 16,000 men. Cornwallis wrote to the British to ask for more soldiers.

16

American soldiers marched from Rhode Island to Yorktown, Virginia. They knew that the British had a fort in Yorktown.

17

Americans Trap British at Yorktown

By October 1781, General Washington and his French allies controlled all of the **routes** into Yorktown, Virginia. The American and French armies surrounded the British fort on land. French admiral

18

de Grasse and his navy controlled the bay. On October 6, 1781, the Americans began the siege against the British. They shot at the British fort with guns and cannons until the walls crumbled.

British general Cornwallis did not have enough soldiers or weapons to fight. He was running out of food. He kept asking for more soldiers. A British fleet sailed south to help him and his soldiers. It was too late. On October 19, General Cornwallis asked the Americans for a **truce**.

This picture shows General Washington and General Rochambeau standing on top of a trench in Yorktown.

19

British Surrender to Americans

On October 19, 1781, British general Charles Cornwallis agreed to surrender his army of 7,157 men to American general George Washington. The Americans waited for the British to come out of the fort.

Cornwallis did not come out. Another British general named Charles O'Hara led the British from the fort instead. He said that General Cornwallis was sick. General O'Hara tried to surrender to the French. The British had once ruled the American colonists. They did not want to admit that they had lost the war to the Americans. The French made General O'Hara surrender to the Americans.

On October 19, 1781, the British surrendered to the Americans at Yorktown. This marked the end of the Revolutionary War.

20

21

American Colonies Become States

The British government found out about the British army's surrender at Yorktown. They knew England could not win the war. The British decided to make peace with the colonists. They went to Paris, France, to write a peace agreement. The British and the Americans wrote the final agreement on April 15, 1783. This agreement was called the **Treaty** of Paris.

The Treaty of Paris gave the Americans all of the land between the Atlantic Ocean and the Mississippi River, north to Canada and south to Florida. It made the 13 colonies into 13 free and **independent** states. The Americans could now form their own government and make their own laws.

GLOSSARY

allies (A-lyz) Groups of people that agree to help another group of people.

colonies (KAH-luh-neez) Areas in a new country where large groups of people move, who are still ruled by the leaders and laws of their old countries.

fleet (FLEET) Many ships under the command of one person.

fort (FORT) A strong building or place that can be defended against an enemy.

independent (in-dih-PEN-dint) Free from the control, support, or help of other people.

messengers (MEH–sin-jurz) People who deliver messages.

retreat (ree-TREET) To back away from a fight.

routes (ROOTS) Paths you take to get somewhere.

siege (SEEJ) A strong attack.

subjects (SUB-jekts) People who are ruled by a king or a government.

surrender (suh-REN-der) To give up to an enemy.

treaty (TREE-tee) A formal agreement, especially one between nations, signed and agreed upon by both nations.

trenches (TRENCH-ez) Long pits dug in the ground where soldiers hide to shoot at an enemy.

truce (TROOS) An agreement to end a battle or a war.

wilderness (WIL-dur-nis) An area that is wild and has no permanent settlements.

23

INDEX

C

Cornwallis, General
Charles, 8, 9, 13, 14,
16, 19, 20

F

Ferguson, Patrick, 11

G

Gates, General Horatio, 8
George III, King, 5

Grasse, Admiral de, 7, 14,
19
Greene, Nathanael, 12,
13

L

Lafayette, General, 7, 14

M

Marion, Francis, 10
Morgan, Daniel, 13

O

O'Hara, General Charles,
20

R

Rochambeau, General, 7,
14, 16

W

Washington, General
George, 7, 14, 16,
18, 20

WEB SITES

To learn more about the Battle of Yorktown, check out these Web sites:

http://www.geocites.com/Heartland/Ranch/9198/rwarproj/Yorktown.htm
http://members.aol.com/spursfan50/davidallen/yorktown.htm